CONTENTS

The Cryptid Files   1

Summary: 2

Introduction to the Pacific Northwest's Bigfoot   3

Chapter 1: The Legend of Bigfoot - The History of Sasquatch Sightings   6

Chapter 2: Sasquatch Sightings in the Pacific Northwest   12

Chapter 3: Scientific Investigations   20

Chapter 4: Myths and Legends   26

Chapter 5: The Debate over Bigfoot's Existence   33

Chapter 6: The Elusive Sasquatch   40

Chapter 7: Sasquatch in Popular Culture   47

Chapter 8: Famous Sasquatch Sightings   54

Chapter 9: Final Thoughts and Conclusions   60

THE CRYPTID FILES

Legends and Lore of the Pacific Northwest's Bigfoot.

SUMMARY:

Join us on a thrilling journey through the Pacific Northwest's dense forests and remote wilderness as we explore the mysteries of the legendary Sasquatch, better known as Bigfoot. Through first-hand accounts and in-depth research, we examine the evidence and legends surrounding this elusive creature, shedding light on one of the world's most intriguing mysteries.

INTRODUCTION TO THE PACIFIC NORTHWEST'S BIGFOOT

In the dense forests and rugged mountains of the Pacific Northwest, there exists a creature that has captured the imagination of people for generations. Known as Sasquatch or Bigfoot, this elusive cryptid has been the subject of countless stories, sightings, and investigations.
The Bigfoot is believed to be a large, hairy, bipedal creature standing up to 10 feet tall and weighing up to 1,000 pounds. Its footprint, measuring up to 24 inches in length, is distinctive and has been found all over the region. While there is no concrete evidence to prove its existence, many people firmly believe in its presence, and its legend has become a significant part of the region's culture.

The stories of the Bigfoot have been passed down through generations of Indigenous tribes in the Pacific Northwest. Many tribes have their own name and unique descriptions of the creature. They believe it to be a spiritual being and have various tales and legends that involve the Bigfoot.

In recent years, researchers and enthusiasts have taken an interest in studying Bigfoot sightings, collecting evidence, and investigating alleged encounters. While some dismiss it as a mere myth or folklore, others believe there is much more to the story and continue to search for the truth.

This book, "Sasquatch Stories: Legends and Lore of the Pacific Northwest's Bigfoot," delves into the fascinating history, stories, and sightings of this elusive creature. From the earliest Indigenous legends to modern-day sightings and investigations, we explore the enduring mystery of the Bigfoot and its place in Pacific Northwest folklore.

CHAPTER 1:
THE LEGEND
OF BIGFOOT -
THE HISTORY
OF SASQUATCH
SIGHTINGS

The Pacific Northwest has been home to many mysteries, but none so famous as the elusive creature known as Bigfoot. Also known as Sasquatch, this legendary creature has been the subject of fascination for centuries, with stories and sightings dating back to the Native American tribes who first inhabited the region.

The legend of Bigfoot has been passed down through generations, with tales of a large, hairy, ape-like creature that roams the forests and mountains of the Pacific Northwest. The first written account of a Sasquatch sighting was recorded in 1811 by a British explorer named David Thompson, who encountered large footprints in what is now the state of Washington.

Since then, there have been countless reported sightings of Sasquatch throughout the Pacific Northwest, with many of them concentrated in the dense forests of Washington, Oregon, and British Columbia. These sightings have come from all walks of life, from hikers and hunters to loggers and park rangers.

Despite the abundance of sightings, physical evidence of Sasquatch remains elusive. While there have been numerous alleged footprints, hair samples, and even videos and photographs, none of this evidence has been conclusively proven to be from a real Sasquatch.

Despite the lack of definitive proof, the legend of Bigfoot continues to captivate people's imaginations and inspire countless books, movies, and TV shows. Some people believe that Sasquatch is simply a myth or legend, while others are convinced that it is a real, undiscovered species that roams the forests of the Pacific Northwest.

Regardless of where you stand on the existence of Sasquatch, there is no denying the impact that this legendary creature has had on popular culture and the imagination of people around the world.

Over the years, there have been numerous encounters with Bigfoot reported, some more famous than others. One of the most famous occurred in 1967 when Roger Patterson and Bob Gimlin captured what is arguably the most famous footage of Bigfoot ever taken, known as the Patterson-Gimlin film. The footage shows a large, bipedal creature walking through the woods in Northern California, turning to look back at the camera before disappearing into the trees. The footage has been analyzed and debated for years, with some believing it to be a hoax and others convinced it's the real deal.

Another well-known encounter happened in 1924,

when a group of miners in Ape Canyon, Washington claimed to have been attacked by a group of Sasquatch. The miners claimed that the creatures threw rocks at their cabin and attempted to break in while they were inside. They fired their weapons at the creatures, but claimed they were impervious to the bullets. The story has since become a famous legend in the Pacific Northwest and has been the subject of many books, movies, and documentaries.

There have also been many other reported sightings and encounters with Bigfoot throughout the years, including accounts of vocalizations, footprints, and even close-up sightings. While skeptics may dismiss these reports as hoaxes or misidentifications of other animals, many people believe in the existence of Bigfoot and continue to search for evidence of its existence.

For decades, researchers and enthusiasts have been searching for evidence of Bigfoot, a mysterious creature that is said to inhabit the dense forests of the Pacific Northwest. While many sightings of Bigfoot have been reported over the years, the scientific community has largely remained skeptical about its existence, citing a lack of physical evidence.

Despite this, numerous researchers have dedicated their lives to studying and researching Bigfoot, hoping to uncover proof of its existence. In this chapter, we will provide a brief overview of some of the most notable research efforts and findings related to Bigfoot.

One of the earliest and most famous Bigfoot researchers was a man named Rene Dahinden. In the 1950s, Dahinden became interested in the creature after hearing reports of sightings from hunters and loggers in the Pacific Northwest. He spent much of his life searching for Bigfoot, collecting evidence and interviewing witnesses in an effort to prove the creature's existence.

Another prominent Bigfoot researcher was Dr. Grover Krantz, a physical anthropologist who believed that Bigfoot was a real animal species that had yet to be discovered by science. Krantz spent years studying alleged Bigfoot footprints and collected casts of hundreds of prints. He also performed detailed analyses of alleged Bigfoot hair samples, attempting to determine if they belonged to an unknown species.

In recent years, DNA testing has emerged as a powerful tool in Bigfoot research. In 2012, a group of researchers led by Dr. Melba Ketchum claimed to have analyzed DNA samples from purported Bigfoot hair and tissue samples, finding that they belonged to an unknown hominid species. However, this claim has been met with skepticism from many in the scientific community, who have questioned the validity of the DNA samples and the testing methods used.

Despite the lack of definitive evidence, interest in Bigfoot remains high, with numerous Bigfoot organizations and research groups still actively investigating reports of sightings and collecting evidence in the hopes of one day proving the creature's existence. In the following chapters, we will delve deeper into the legends and lore surrounding Bigfoot, as well as some of the most compelling sightings and encounters that have been reported over the years.

CHAPTER 2: SASQUATCH SIGHTINGS IN THE PACIFIC NORTHWEST

Reports from Washington State

Washington State is known for its dense forests,

towering mountains, and rugged coastline. It's also known for being one of the hotspots for Bigfoot sightings. For decades, eyewitnesses have reported seeing Sasquatch in the Pacific Northwest, and Washington State has more sightings per capita than any other state in the United States.

The first reported sighting of Sasquatch in Washington State occurred in 1924 when a group of miners in Ape Canyon claimed they were attacked by a group of creatures resembling apes. The miners reported seeing footprints measuring 14 inches in length and claimed the creatures threw rocks at their cabin. They managed to fend off the creatures with gunfire and escaped unharmed.

Since then, there have been countless reports of Sasquatch sightings in Washington State. In 1969, a man named Fred Beck claimed he and his mining crew were attacked by Sasquatch in the same area of Ape Canyon. Beck claimed the creatures threw rocks at them and even broke into their cabin. This encounter became known as the "Battle of Ape Canyon."

In 1971, a man named Dwayne Pintoff captured footage of what appeared to be a Sasquatch near the town of Granite Falls. The footage shows a large, hairy creature walking through a wooded area before disappearing from view.

In 1994, a woman named Cinnamon Brown

reported seeing a Sasquatch on the Olympic Peninsula. Brown claimed the creature was standing on its hind legs and was over 8 feet tall. She also reported hearing strange vocalizations that she believed were coming from the Sasquatch.

These are just a few of the many reported sightings of Sasquatch in Washington State. While skeptics dismiss these reports as hoaxes or misidentifications of known animals, many researchers believe that there is something to these sightings and continue to investigate and document encounters with Sasquatch in the Pacific Northwest.

Oregon is another hotspot for Bigfoot sightings, with reports dating back to the early 1900s. One of the most famous incidents occurred in 1967, when Roger Patterson and Bob Gimlin captured what is arguably the most well-known footage of a Bigfoot, known as the Patterson-Gimlin film. The footage shows a large, bipedal creature walking through a clearing in Bluff Creek, California.

Other notable sightings in Oregon include the 2000 encounter of a group of hikers who reported seeing a large, ape-like creature near Mount Hood. In 2013, a hunter in Josephine County reported seeing a Bigfoot near the Rogue River, and in 2014, a woman driving on Highway 97 claimed to have seen a Sasquatch crossing the road.

Sightings have continued into recent years, with

several reports coming out of the Umpqua National Forest in southwestern Oregon. One of the most intriguing sightings was reported in 2019 by a woman who claimed to have seen a Bigfoot standing on a log in the forest.

Despite the numerous reports and evidence, many skeptics remain unconvinced and attribute the sightings to misidentification, hoaxes, or other natural explanations. Nevertheless, Sasquatch continues to capture the imagination and curiosity of people around the world.

British Columbia, Canada, is known for its vast wilderness and rugged terrain, making it a prime location for Sasquatch sightings. The province has a long history of Bigfoot sightings, with reports dating back to the early 1800s.

One of the most famous Sasquatch sightings in British Columbia occurred in 1924 near Harrison Hot Springs. A group of workers clearing land for a railway claimed to have seen a large, hair-covered creature standing on two legs. The creature reportedly let out a terrifying scream before running off into the woods.

In 1957, a man named William Roe claimed to have encountered a female Sasquatch while he was hunting in the forests near Toba Inlet. Roe described the creature as being about seven feet tall, with dark hair covering its entire body. He reported that the

Sasquatch made a series of guttural sounds before turning and disappearing into the forest.

More recent sightings have been reported in areas such as Mission, Squamish, and Harrison Mills. In 2017, a group of hikers claimed to have captured video footage of a Sasquatch in the mountains near Squamish. The footage, which quickly went viral, shows a large, dark figure moving through the trees.

These are just a few examples of the many Sasquatch sightings that have occurred in British Columbia over the years. The province remains a hotbed of Bigfoot activity, with researchers and enthusiasts continuing to investigate reported sightings and search for evidence of the elusive creature's existence.

While sightings of Bigfoot have occurred all over the world, the Pacific Northwest has been a hotbed of activity for decades. With so many reported sightings in the area, it's no surprise that a dedicated group of researchers has emerged, determined to prove the existence of this elusive creature.

In this chapter, we'll take a look at some of the most popular research techniques used to search for Sasquatch.

Methods for Searching for Sasquatch:

Footprint Analysis: One of the most common methods of Bigfoot research is the analysis of footprints. Researchers will cast or make a plaster impression of a footprint and use the size and shape of the print to estimate the size and weight of the creature. They can also analyze the depth and pattern of the footprints to determine the creature's gait.

Audio Recordings: Many Bigfoot researchers believe that the creature communicates through vocalizations, such as whoops, growls, and screams. Researchers will often use audio recording equipment to capture these sounds and analyze them for patterns or clues about the creature's behavior.

Trail Cameras: Trail cameras are a popular tool for Bigfoot researchers, as they can be set up in remote locations to capture footage of the creature. Researchers will often bait the area around the camera with food or other objects to entice the creature to come closer.

Tools of the Trade:

Night Vision Goggles: Many researchers believe that Bigfoot is primarily active at night, making night vision goggles a valuable tool for spotting the creature in the dark.

Flir Cameras: Flir cameras use thermal imaging to detect heat signatures, making them a valuable tool for researchers trying to spot Bigfoot in heavily forested areas.

Technology and the Hunt for Bigfoot:

Drones: Drones have become an increasingly popular tool for Bigfoot researchers, allowing them to explore remote or inaccessible areas from the air.

DNA Analysis: With advances in DNA analysis, researchers can now test hair, saliva, and other samples thought to belong to Bigfoot for genetic material. While the results of these tests have been inconclusive so far, they offer a promising avenue for future research.

By using these research techniques, tools, and technologies, Bigfoot researchers hope to gather evidence that will finally prove the existence of this mysterious creature.

Some researchers and enthusiasts have turned to advanced technology to aid them in their search for Bigfoot. In recent years, drones have become increasingly popular among Sasquatch hunters. Drones equipped with cameras and thermal imaging technology allow researchers to search areas that are difficult to access on foot or from the air.

Another tool that has gained popularity in recent years is trail cameras. These motion-activated cameras can be set up in remote areas to capture images of wildlife, including Bigfoot. Some researchers have claimed to have captured photos and videos of Bigfoot using trail cameras.

In addition to technology, there are also more traditional methods that are used in Bigfoot research. One such method is plaster casting of footprints. When researchers find what they believe to be Bigfoot footprints, they can create a plaster cast of the print to preserve it for further analysis.

Finally, some researchers have turned to baiting as a method for attracting Bigfoot. This involves leaving food or other items in areas where Bigfoot sightings have been reported, in the hopes that the creature will be lured in by the scent and leave behind evidence such as footprints or hair samples.

While there is no guarantee that any of these methods will lead to a Bigfoot sighting or capture, they all play a role in the ongoing search for Sasquatch.

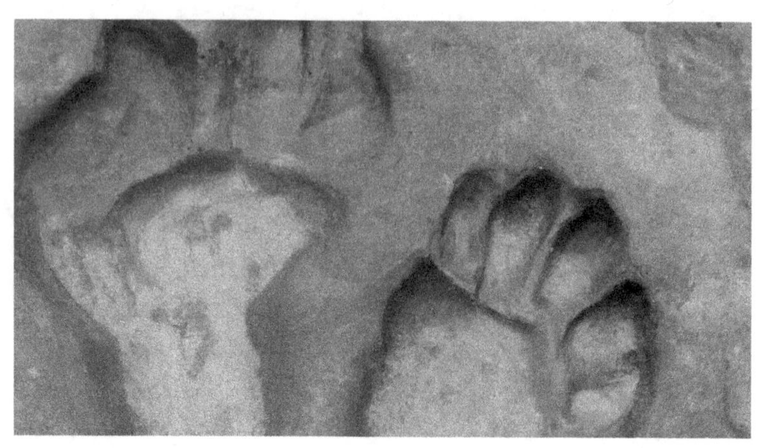

CHAPTER 3:
SCIENTIFIC
INVESTIGATIONS

Despite being widely regarded as a cryptid, the Sasquatch has been the subject of scientific investigation for many years. While some researchers dismiss Bigfoot as mere myth, others believe there may be some truth to the sightings and reports. In this chapter, we will explore some of the scientific studies conducted on Sasquatch, the criticisms and skepticism surrounding them, and current theories about this elusive creature.

Scientific Studies of the Sasquatch:

Over the years, there have been a number of scientific investigations into the existence of Sasquatch. In the 1960s and 1970s, the most famous of these was the work of anthropologist Grover Krantz. Krantz believed that Bigfoot was a relic hominid, related to Gigantopithecus, an extinct ape from Asia. Krantz's work focused on the physical evidence of Sasquatch, such as footprints and hair samples.

In more recent times, DNA analysis has been used to try and identify the source of alleged Sasquatch hair samples. One such study was conducted by Dr. Melba Ketchum, a veterinarian and DNA researcher. Her study claimed to have found genetic evidence of a new hominin species, but the results were heavily criticized by the scientific community and remain controversial.

Criticisms and Skepticism:

While some scientists have conducted serious research into Sasquatch, others dismiss the idea of Bigfoot outright. One of the main criticisms of Bigfoot research is the lack of physical evidence.

While there have been many sightings and reports of Sasquatch, no one has ever captured a live specimen or found a dead one. Critics argue that without hard evidence, Sasquatch cannot be considered a real creature.

Another criticism of Bigfoot research is the lack of reproducibility. Many of the techniques used by researchers, such as wood knocking and vocalizations, cannot be scientifically tested or replicated.

Current Theories about Sasquatch:

Despite the skepticism surrounding Bigfoot research, many continue to believe that there may be something to the reports of Sasquatch sightings. Some researchers suggest that Bigfoot may be a surviving relic population of Gigantopithecus or a similar prehistoric ape. Others speculate that Sasquatch is a new species of hominid, related to humans but evolved separately.

In recent years, there has been growing interest in the possibility that Sasquatch could be a type of undiscovered primate. Some researchers have suggested that Sasquatch may be related to the Orangutan, due to similarities in their physical characteristics and behavior.

Despite decades of research, the question of whether Sasquatch exists or not remains unresolved. While some researchers continue to study Bigfoot, others remain skeptical of its existence. Regardless of whether or not Bigfoot is ever proven to be real, the legend of this mysterious creature is likely to continue to capture the imagination of people around the world.

In recent years, there have been several scientific investigations into the existence of Bigfoot, with researchers using DNA analysis and other advanced techniques to try and find evidence of its existence. However, many scientists remain skeptical of the creature's existence, citing the lack of concrete evidence and the high number of hoaxes and misidentifications associated with reported sightings.

Despite the skepticism, there are some researchers who believe that Bigfoot is a real, living creature that has managed to elude detection for centuries. One popular theory is that Bigfoot is a surviving relic hominid, a primitive human-like species that went extinct millions of years ago, but somehow managed to survive in isolated pockets of the world.

Another theory is that Bigfoot is a form of undiscovered primate, related to the great apes such as gorillas and chimpanzees. Supporters of this theory point to the many reported sightings of Bigfoot that describe the creature as having human-like characteristics, such as the ability to walk on two legs and use its hands to manipulate objects.

Regardless of the current scientific opinions, the legend of Bigfoot remains a popular and enduring part of American folklore. And with new advances in technology and continued research, who knows what secrets the forests of the Pacific Northwest might still hold.

While some researchers have attempted to provide scientific evidence for the existence of the Skunk Ape, the scientific community as a whole remains largely skeptical. Critics argue that there is a lack of hard evidence to support the existence of this creature, such as bones, hair, or DNA samples.

Some skeptics have suggested that sightings of the Skunk Ape may actually be misidentifications of other animals or even hoaxes perpetrated by individuals seeking attention or profit. Others argue that the phenomenon may be the result of folklore and urban legends that have been passed down through generations.

Despite the criticisms and skepticism, many individuals and organizations continue to investigate the Skunk Ape and other cryptids. Some researchers use advanced technology, such as drones and infrared cameras, to try to capture images of the elusive creature. Others use more traditional methods, such as plaster casting footprints and interviewing eyewitnesses.

As research on the Skunk Ape and other cryptids

continues, theories about the nature and origins of these creatures continue to evolve. Some researchers suggest that they may be surviving members of ancient species, while others propose that they may be the result of genetic mutations or adaptations to their environments. Still others suggest that they may be extradimensional beings or even extraterrestrial in origin.

Despite the ongoing debates and controversies, the legend of the Skunk Ape remains a fascinating and enduring part of American folklore and popular culture.

CHAPTER 4:
MYTHS AND
LEGENDS

As with any enigmatic creature, myths and legends have arisen around Bigfoot, adding to its mysterious and captivating aura. In this chapter, we will explore some of the most popular myths and legends surrounding Bigfoot.

Bigfoot is an aggressive and dangerous creature.

One of the most enduring myths about Bigfoot is that it is a violent and unpredictable creature. However, this perception is not supported by evidence. In fact, there have been very few reports of Bigfoot behaving aggressively towards humans.

Bigfoot is a supernatural being.

Some people believe that Bigfoot is not a flesh-and-blood creature, but rather a supernatural being or interdimensional traveler. This belief is based on reports of Bigfoot seemingly appearing and disappearing without a trace, and the creature's supposed ability to elude capture.

Bigfoot is a missing link between humans and apes.

Another popular theory is that Bigfoot is a missing link between humans and apes. This theory is based on the physical similarities between Bigfoot and other primates, as well as reports of Bigfoot exhibiting human-like behaviors such as using tools and building structures.

Bigfoot is an alien or extraterrestrial.

Some people believe that Bigfoot is not of this world, but rather an alien or extraterrestrial creature. This theory is based on reports of UFO sightings in areas where Bigfoot has been spotted, as well as the idea that Bigfoot's abilities (such as invisibility and teleportation) are beyond the capabilities of any earthly creature.

Bigfoot is a spirit or guardian of the wilderness.

In some Native American cultures, Bigfoot is viewed as a spirit or guardian of the wilderness. According to legend, Bigfoot helps lost travelers find their way back to safety and protects the natural environment from harm.

While there is no scientific evidence to support these myths and legends, they continue to fascinate and inspire people to search for Bigfoot and unravel the mysteries surrounding this elusive creature.

Folklore Surrounding Bigfoot:

Bigfoot, being a part of indigenous cultures and their folklore, has been associated with several legends and myths. These legends vary from one culture to another and offer insight into the way Bigfoot was perceived by these communities.

One of the most popular myths is that Bigfoot is a gentle creature who is more afraid of humans than we are of him. Many Native American cultures believe that Bigfoot is a spiritual guardian of the forest and that he only appears to those who have pure intentions.

In some cultures, Bigfoot is seen as a trickster who likes to play pranks on humans. In others, he is believed to be a bringer of good luck and prosperity.

One Native American legend tells the story of how Bigfoot helped a hunter who had lost his way in the forest. According to the legend, the hunter stumbled upon Bigfoot's home and was welcomed by the creature. Bigfoot then showed the hunter the way back to his village and even gave him a magical talisman to protect him from harm.

Another legend from the Pacific Northwest tells of a tribe that made a deal with Bigfoot. In exchange for leaving their village alone, the tribe promised to leave food out for Bigfoot every night. The tribe honored their promise, and Bigfoot kept his word by never disturbing the village.

These legends and myths are an important part of Bigfoot's cultural significance and offer a glimpse into the way indigenous cultures viewed this mysterious creature.

Throughout history, many myths and legends have developed around the Sasquatch or Bigfoot. Native American cultures have rich folklore surrounding these creatures, often depicting them as powerful and mysterious beings with spiritual significance.

For example, the Salish tribes of the Pacific Northwest believe in a creature known as the "Ts'emekwes," which they describe as a large, hairy, man-like creature that lives in the mountains. They believe that the Ts'emekwes is a guardian of the natural world and has the power to heal and bring good fortune.

The Lummi people of Washington state tell stories of a Sasquatch-like creature known as "Guguyni," which they believe is a benevolent spirit that watches over the forest and its inhabitants.

Similarly, the Sts'ailes people of British Columbia have a legend about a creature known as "Sásq'ets," which they describe as a giant, hairy, and powerful being that can move through the forest without leaving a trace. They believe that Sásq'ets is a guardian of the land and has the power to grant wishes and bring good luck.

In popular culture, Bigfoot has also been depicted in various ways, from a gentle, misunderstood creature to a terrifying monster. Films such as "Harry and the Hendersons" and "The Legend of Boggy Creek" have portrayed Bigfoot in a more sympathetic light, while horror films like "Sasquatch" and "Exists" have depicted them as dangerous and bloodthirsty.

Despite the many myths and legends surrounding Bigfoot, the true nature of these creatures remains a mystery, and scientists continue to investigate and study them to uncover the truth behind the legend.

Bigfoot has become an icon in pop culture,

appearing in movies, TV shows, books, and even commercials. The image of the giant, hairy creature lurking in the woods has captured the imagination of people around the world. Here are some examples of Bigfoot's influence on popular culture:

"Harry and the Hendersons" - This 1987 film tells the story of a family who adopts a friendly Bigfoot named Harry. The movie was a box office success and spawned a short-lived TV series.

"Finding Bigfoot" - This reality TV show, which aired from 2011 to 2018, followed a team of Bigfoot researchers as they traveled the world in search of the elusive creature.

Bigfoot in Music - Bigfoot has been the subject of many songs, from the folk ballad "The Legend of Bigfoot" by Steve Wozniak to the heavy metal anthem "Sasquatch" by Tenacious D.

Bigfoot in Advertising - Bigfoot has been used to sell everything from beef jerky to beer. One famous commercial for Jack Link's Beef Jerky features a man being chased by a Bigfoot who wants to steal his snack.

Bigfoot in Art - Bigfoot has inspired many artists, from comic book illustrators to painters. Some notable examples include the "Bigfoot Lives!" mural in Portland, Oregon and the bronze statue of Bigfoot in Willow Creek, California.

The fascination with Bigfoot in popular culture has only grown over the years, and it's clear that the legend of the Sasquatch will continue to captivate people for generations to come.

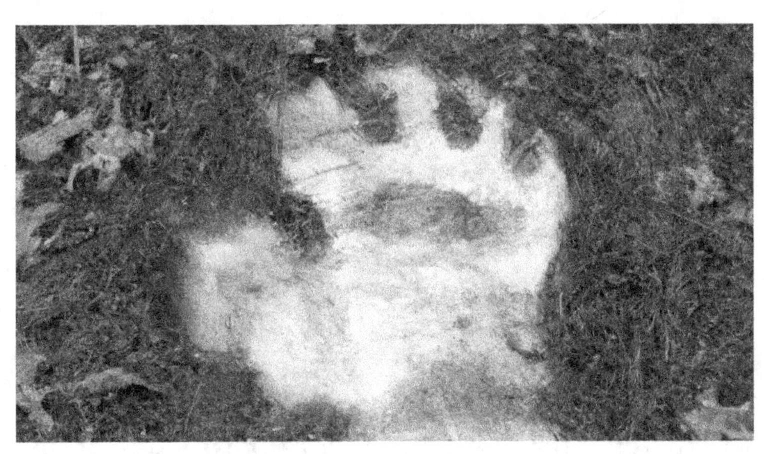

CHAPTER 5: THE DEBATE OVER BIGFOOT'S EXISTENCE

The existence of Bigfoot or Sasquatch has been a topic of debate for decades. While some people believe in its existence based on sighting reports, footprints, and other pieces of evidence, others argue that there is no concrete evidence to support the idea of Bigfoot's existence. In this chapter, we will explore both sides of the debate and the arguments put forth by skeptics and believers.

Believers argue that there is ample evidence to support the existence of Bigfoot, including hundreds of sighting reports, footprints, and even video footage. Some researchers have dedicated their lives to studying Bigfoot and have claimed to have seen or heard the creature themselves. Believers also point to the fact that there are similar legends and sightings of similar creatures around the world, such as the Yeti in the Himalayas or the Yowie in Australia.

Skeptics, on the other hand, argue that there is no concrete evidence to support the existence of Bigfoot. They claim that the sighting reports and footprints can be explained by misidentification or hoaxes, and that the lack of physical evidence, such as bones or DNA, is suspicious. Some critics argue that the idea of Bigfoot is simply a modern-day myth or legend, perpetuated by pop culture and the media.

Despite the lack of conclusive evidence, the debate over Bigfoot's existence continues to attract the attention of researchers and enthusiasts alike. Some argue that even if Bigfoot doesn't exist, the search for it has led to valuable discoveries about wildlife and the natural world. Others maintain that the possibility of Bigfoot's existence is worth pursuing, and that we may one day discover conclusive evidence of its existence.

The Skeptics' Perspective

The skeptics' perspective on the existence of Bigfoot centers around the lack of concrete evidence. Despite decades of reported sightings, footprints, and other anecdotal evidence, there has never been a verifiable Bigfoot specimen captured or studied by mainstream science.

Critics argue that the supposed Bigfoot sightings are often misidentifications of known animals or outright hoaxes. For example, some researchers have suggested that many reported Bigfoot sightings are simply sightings of bears or other large mammals in the woods. Others argue that footprints and other supposed evidence of Bigfoot could have been created through natural means, such as wind or erosion, or even by human pranksters.

Skeptics also point to the lack of corroborating evidence from other sources, such as hair or DNA samples. While some researchers have claimed to have found hair or other physical evidence that could be linked to Bigfoot, these claims have typically been met with skepticism and have not been widely accepted by the scientific community.

Despite the skepticism, many believers in Bigfoot argue that the lack of evidence does not necessarily prove that the creature does not exist. They point out that many animal species have remained undiscovered until relatively recently, and that the vast and remote forests of the Pacific Northwest and other areas could easily harbor a large, undiscovered primate species.

The debate over Bigfoot's existence is likely to continue for years to come, with passionate arguments on both sides. Ultimately, the question of whether Bigfoot exists may never be definitively answered, but the ongoing search for evidence and exploration of the legend will undoubtedly continue to capture the imaginations of many people around the world.

The Proponents' Argument

While skeptics often criticize Bigfoot research for being unscientific, proponents of Bigfoot's existence argue that there is ample evidence to suggest that the creature is real. Here are some of the key arguments put forth by those who believe in the existence of Bigfoot:

Eyewitness Reports: One of the most compelling arguments in favor of Bigfoot's existence is the large number of eyewitness reports that have been collected over the years. These reports come from people of all walks of life, from hunters and outdoors enthusiasts to ordinary citizens going about their daily lives. Many of these reports describe similar physical characteristics and behaviors, suggesting that there may indeed be a common creature behind the sightings.

Physical Evidence: While skeptics often dismiss physical evidence as unreliable or inconclusive, proponents of Bigfoot point to a number of pieces of evidence that they believe suggest the creature's existence. Footprints are perhaps the most famous form of physical evidence associated with Bigfoot, and there have been many casts made of what appear to be large, bipedal footprints that could not have been made by a human or any known animal. In addition, there have been reports of hair samples, scat, and even DNA evidence that some researchers believe could be linked to Bigfoot.

Historical Accounts: Proponents of Bigfoot also point to historical accounts of similar creatures found in cultures around the world. For example, in North America, indigenous peoples have long told stories of creatures that resemble Bigfoot. Similar creatures have been reported in other parts of the world, from the Yeti of the Himalayas to the Yowie of Australia.

Audio Recordings: Another type of evidence often cited by Bigfoot researchers is audio recordings of vocalizations that are said to resemble Bigfoot calls. While skeptics argue that these recordings could be hoaxes or could be attributed to known animals, proponents of Bigfoot point to the distinctive nature of the sounds as evidence that they could not have been made by any known animal.

In summary, proponents of Bigfoot argue that the sheer volume of eyewitness reports, physical evidence, historical accounts, and audio recordings provide compelling evidence that there is a large, bipedal primate living in the forests of North America. While skeptics may argue that this evidence is insufficient or unreliable, many researchers continue to search for definitive proof of Bigfoot's existence.

The debate over Bigfoot's existence is likely to continue for years to come. While skeptics point to the lack of concrete evidence as proof that Bigfoot is nothing more than a myth, proponents argue that there is enough circumstantial evidence to suggest that there may be something out there.

Despite the controversy, interest in Bigfoot remains high, and new sightings and reports continue to be documented each year. As technology and research techniques continue to evolve, it is possible that more concrete evidence may be uncovered in the future.

In recent years, DNA analysis has been used to investigate alleged Bigfoot hair samples, with some researchers claiming that they have found evidence of an unknown primate species. Others have turned to drone technology to search for evidence in areas that would be difficult or dangerous for humans to access.

It is also possible that as more people venture into remote wilderness areas, the chances of encountering a Sasquatch will increase. With the advent of social media, it is easier than ever for individuals to share their stories and sightings with a wide audience, leading to greater awareness and interest in Bigfoot.

Regardless of whether Bigfoot is ever proven to be real, the legend and lore of the Sasquatch will continue to captivate the imaginations of people around the world.

CHAPTER 6:
THE ELUSIVE SASQUATCH

Despite the many reported sightings, Bigfoot remains a highly elusive creature. In this chapter, we will explore some of the reasons why it has been so difficult to conclusively prove the existence of Sasquatch.

One of the main reasons why Bigfoot has been so difficult to find is that it appears to be highly skilled at avoiding human contact. There are a number of theories as to why this might be the case. Some researchers believe that Bigfoot is highly intelligent and has developed a range of sophisticated behaviors to avoid detection. For example, it is thought that Bigfoot is highly skilled at moving silently through the forest, and that it may be able to sense human presence from a distance.

Others believe that Bigfoot has simply adapted to the presence of humans over time. It is thought that the creature may have learned to avoid areas of high human activity, and to only venture out into the open during periods of low human activity. Some researchers also believe that Bigfoot may be highly nocturnal, and that it spends most of its time hiding during the day.

Another factor that makes Bigfoot difficult to find is its physical characteristics. Unlike other large animals, such as bears or deer, Bigfoot is not typically seen out in the open. Instead, it is often spotted moving through dense forest, making it difficult to observe its full physical form. Additionally, Bigfoot appears to be highly adept at hiding its tracks, which makes it difficult to follow.

Finally, one of the major challenges facing Bigfoot researchers is the limited funding available for this type of research. Compared to other areas of scientific research, Bigfoot research is often seen as a niche area, and funding for research projects is limited. This can make it difficult for researchers to carry out the kind of long-term, large-scale studies that are needed to conclusively prove the existence of Bigfoot.

Despite the challenges, many researchers remain optimistic that one day we will be able to conclusively prove the existence of Bigfoot. Whether through the development of new research techniques, increased funding, or simply through continued persistence and dedication, it is clear that the search for Sasquatch is far from over.

The elusive nature of Bigfoot has made it difficult for researchers to study and understand its habits and behaviors. However, there have been various theories and hypotheses put forward over the years based on reported sightings and evidence.

One theory is that Bigfoot is a nocturnal creature that primarily hunts and moves at night. This would explain why many sightings occur during the early morning or late evening hours. Another theory is that Bigfoot is a migratory species that travels vast distances in search of food and shelter. Some researchers have even suggested that Bigfoot may have the ability to hibernate during the winter months, similar to bears.

In terms of behavior, there have been reports

of Bigfoot exhibiting both aggressive and passive behavior. Some witnesses have reported being chased or even attacked by Bigfoot, while others have claimed to observe Bigfoot simply watching them from a distance. Some researchers have suggested that Bigfoot may have a social structure similar to that of primates, with hierarchical relationships and family groups.

Overall, the study of Bigfoot's habits and behaviors remains largely speculative, as there is limited scientific data available to support any particular theory. However, continued research and investigation may help shed light on this elusive creature and its mysterious ways.

Possible Explanations for the Elusiveness of Sasquatch:

Despite decades of research, Bigfoot remains a mystery to the scientific community. Some researchers believe that Bigfoot is so elusive because it is an intelligent and cautious animal, while others suggest that it may have supernatural abilities that allow it to avoid detection. Here are some of the most popular theories about why Sasquatch remains so hard to find:

Stealth and Camouflage: Many Sasquatch sightings occur in heavily wooded areas, where the creature's brown or black fur blends in with the surrounding foliage. Additionally, Bigfoot is often described as being incredibly quiet, with researchers speculating that it may have evolved to move silently through the forest in order to avoid detection.

Intelligence and Caution: Some researchers believe that Sasquatch is an intelligent and cautious animal that has learned to avoid humans over time. For example, it has been suggested that Bigfoot may have observed humans from a distance and learned to avoid their presence in order to protect itself.

Territorial Behavior: Sasquatch may be territorial and stay within a specific area or range. This would make it difficult to track or observe, as it would quickly flee or hide if it sensed the presence of humans.

Supernatural Abilities: Some Bigfoot enthusiasts suggest that the creature may possess supernatural abilities that allow it to avoid detection, such as cloaking or teleportation. However, these theories are not widely accepted by the scientific community.

Despite the lack of concrete evidence, Bigfoot remains a fascinating and popular subject for researchers and enthusiasts alike. As technology and research methods continue to improve, it is possible that we may one day uncover the truth about this elusive creature.

The Challenge of Capturing Proof of Bigfoot's

Existence:

Despite numerous sightings and anecdotal evidence, capturing definitive proof of Bigfoot's existence has proven to be a significant challenge for researchers and enthusiasts alike. Some possible explanations for this include the elusive creature's ability to evade detection and hide in remote areas, as well as the vast areas of unexplored wilderness where it is believed to reside.

One of the most significant obstacles to capturing definitive proof of Bigfoot's existence is the lack of physical evidence. While there have been numerous sightings and even alleged encounters with the creature, there has been very little concrete physical evidence collected. Hair samples and footprints have been found, but these have often been dismissed as being from known animals or as hoaxes.

Another challenge in capturing proof of Bigfoot's existence is the sheer size of the areas where it is believed to reside. Much of the reported sightings have taken place in remote, densely wooded areas where it is difficult to navigate and set up surveillance equipment. The terrain can also make it challenging to collect physical evidence or track the creature's movements.

Despite these challenges, many researchers and enthusiasts remain dedicated to finding definitive proof of Bigfoot's existence. New technologies, such as high-tech cameras, drones, and DNA analysis, are being utilized to increase the likelihood of capturing evidence of the elusive creature. Additionally, the continued interest and public fascination with Bigfoot ensure that the search for proof of its existence will continue for years to come.

CHAPTER 7: SASQUATCH IN POPULAR CULTURE

The legendary creature known as Sasquatch or Bigfoot has captured the imagination of people all over the world for decades. Its mystique and elusiveness have made it a favorite topic of discussion in popular culture, appearing in movies, television shows, books, and other forms of entertainment. In this chapter, we will explore the various ways Sasquatch has been depicted in popular culture.

One of the most popular ways that Sasquatch has been depicted in popular culture is through movies and television shows. There have been numerous films featuring the creature, ranging from low-budget horror movies to big-budget blockbusters. Some of the most well-known Sasquatch movies include "Harry and the Hendersons" and "Big Legend".

In addition to movies, Sasquatch has also made appearances in various television shows. It has been the subject of many documentaries and reality shows, such as "Finding Bigfoot" and "Survivorman". It has also been featured in popular animated shows like "South Park" and "Family Guy".

Sasquatch has also been a popular subject in literature, particularly in the horror and science fiction genres. There are countless books that feature the creature as the main antagonist, such as "The Legend of Bigfoot" by Don Hunter and Rene Dahinden and "Bigfoot War" by Eric S. Brown. Sasquatch has also made appearances in other works of fiction, such as the "Goosebumps" book "The Abominable Snowman of Pasadena".

Even the music industry has been touched by the Sasquatch phenomenon. There are several songs that reference or are inspired by the creature, such as "Bigfoot" by W&W and "Bigfoot Country" by R.W. Hampton. The band "Bigfoot" even takes its name from the creature.

Sasquatch's status as a cultural icon is evident in its many appearances in popular culture. While its existence may be debated, there is no denying the impact that it has had on the world of entertainment. From movies and television shows to literature and music, Sasquatch's legend lives on in the hearts and minds of people all over the world.

Bigfoot has been a popular subject in film and television for decades. The creature has appeared in numerous documentaries, TV shows, and movies, both as a central character and as a background element. Here are some examples:

"The Legend of Boggy Creek" (1972): This low-budget docudrama about a Sasquatch-like creature terrorizing a small Arkansas town became a cult classic and helped popularize the Bigfoot legend in the 1970s.

"Harry and the Hendersons" (1987): This family-friendly comedy about a suburban family who adopts a friendly Sasquatch won an Academy Award for Best Makeup and spawned a short-lived TV series.

"Finding Bigfoot" (2011-2018): This reality show on Animal Planet followed a team of Bigfoot researchers as they traveled the world in search of the elusive creature.

"Smallfoot" (2018): This animated film tells the story of a Yeti who discovers the existence of humans and challenges the beliefs of his community. Though not strictly a Bigfoot movie, it deals with similar themes.

"Bigfoot Family" (2020): This animated film is a sequel to "Son of Bigfoot" (2017) and follows a teenage boy as he tries to save his Bigfoot father from a mad scientist.

In addition to these examples, Bigfoot has appeared in countless horror movies, mockumentaries, and TV shows over the years. The creature's popularity shows no signs of slowing down, and it's likely that Bigfoot will continue to be a fixture in popular culture for years to come.

Sasquatch has been a popular topic in literature for

many years. Numerous books have been written on the subject, both non-fiction and fiction. Some of the most famous works include:

"Sasquatch: The Apes Among Us" by John Green: This book is considered one of the seminal works on Bigfoot research. Green was a Canadian researcher who spent years collecting stories and accounts of Bigfoot sightings. He compiled his findings into this comprehensive book, which has become a classic in the field.

"The Legend of Bigfoot" by Robert W. Morgan: This book is a fictionalized account of a group of researchers who set out to find the legendary creature. Along the way, they encounter various obstacles and dangers, leading to a thrilling and suspenseful story.

"The Bigfoot Book: The Encyclopedia of Sasquatch, Yeti and Cryptid Primates" by Nick Redfern: This book provides an in-depth look at the world of Bigfoot and other cryptids. It covers the history of sightings and research, as well as popular theories about their origins and behavior.

"Sasquatch: The Search for a North American Wild Man" by Don Hunter and René Dahinden: This book is another classic in the field of Bigfoot research. It chronicles the authors' travels through the Pacific Northwest in search of the elusive creature. Along the way, they encounter numerous witnesses and collect evidence of Bigfoot's existence.

"Bigfoot War" by Eric S. Brown: This novel is a fictionalized account of a group of soldiers who must fight off an army of Sasquatch that have invaded their town. It's a fast-paced and action-packed story that blends horror and military fiction.

These are just a few examples of the many books that have been written about Sasquatch over the years. Whether you're interested in scientific research or fictionalized accounts of encounters with the creature, there's something for everyone in the world of Bigfoot literature.

Bigfoot has become a cultural icon, with a place in popular culture beyond its legend and folklore. Sasquatch has appeared in various forms of media, from films and TV shows to books, comics, and video games.

One of the earliest representations of Bigfoot in popular culture was the 1950 film "The Snow Creature." Since then, numerous films and television shows featuring Bigfoot have been released, including "Harry and the Hendersons," "Smallfoot," and "Bigfoot Family."

Bigfoot has also been a recurring theme in literature, from horror and science fiction to children's books. Some notable examples include "The Bigfoot Book: The Encyclopedia of Sasquatch, Yeti and Cryptid

Primates" by Nick Redfern, "Monstrum: A Dark Fantasy Novel" by Donald James Parker, and "Bigfoot Cinderrrrella" by Tony Johnston.

In addition to its appearances in various media, Bigfoot has also become a popular subject for merchandise, including t-shirts, mugs, and action figures. Bigfoot even has its own holiday, International Bigfoot Day, celebrated every year on the first Saturday in September.

Despite the controversy surrounding its existence, Sasquatch has remained a beloved and enduring cultural figure, captivating audiences with its mystery and intrigue.

CHAPTER 8: FAMOUS SASQUATCH SIGHTINGS

Throughout history, there have been numerous sightings of Sasquatch, many of which have been reported and documented by reputable sources. Here are some of the most famous Sasquatch sightings:

Ape Canyon Attack: In 1924, a group of miners in Ape Canyon, Washington claimed that they were attacked by a group of Sasquatches. The creatures reportedly threw rocks at their cabin and attempted to break in, resulting in a shootout between the miners and the Sasquatches.

Patterson-Gimlin Film: In 1967, Roger Patterson and Bob Gimlin captured what is perhaps the most famous piece of Sasquatch footage ever taken. The film shows what appears to be a female Sasquatch walking through a clearing in Bluff Creek, California.

Skookum Cast: In 2000, a team of researchers in the Gifford Pinchot National Forest in Washington State discovered a set of footprints that appeared to belong to a Sasquatch. The prints were cast in plaster and became known as the Skookum Cast.

Albert Ostman: In 1924, Albert Ostman claimed that he was abducted by a Sasquatch and held captive for several days in British Columbia. He eventually escaped and recounted his story to the public, which helped to popularize the legend of Sasquatch.

Paul Freeman Footage: In 1994, Paul Freeman captured footage of what he claimed to be a Sasquatch in the Blue Mountains of Washington State. The footage shows a large, hairy creature walking through the forest.

Lake Tahoe Footprints: In 2012, a hiker in Lake Tahoe discovered a set of large footprints in the snow that appeared to belong to a Sasquatch. The footprints were over 16 inches long and were spaced over 6 feet apart.

Bauman Incident: In 1924, prospector Albert Bauman claimed that he and his hunting partner were attacked by a Sasquatch in the wilds of Washington State. Bauman claimed that he shot the creature, but it fled and was never found.

These are just a few examples of the many Sasquatch sightings that have been reported over the years. While some people remain skeptical of the existence of Sasquatch, these sightings continue to captivate the public imagination and keep the legend of the elusive creature alive.

There have been many famous Sasquatch sightings over the years, each with its own unique story and set of circumstances. Here are a few more notable encounters with Bigfoot:

The Skookum Cast: In 2000, a group of researchers discovered a strange impression in the mud near the Skookum Meadows area of Washington State. The impression appeared to show the outline of a large, hairy creature lying on its side. The researchers made a cast of the impression, which has become known as the Skookum Cast.

The Patterson-Gimlin Film: Perhaps the most famous piece of evidence for the existence of Bigfoot is the Patterson-Gimlin film. Shot in 1967 in Bluff Creek, California, the film shows what appears to be a large, bipedal creature walking through the woods. Although many skeptics have attempted to debunk the film, it remains one of the most compelling pieces of evidence for Bigfoot's existence.

The Marble Mountain Footage: In 2011, a man named Randy Savig captured what he claimed to be footage of Bigfoot while hiking in the Marble Mountains of California. The video shows a large, dark figure moving through the woods, and has been the subject of much debate among Bigfoot researchers.

The Fouke Monster: In the early 1970s, a creature known as the Fouke Monster began to terrorize the town of Fouke, Arkansas. The creature was described as a large, hairy humanoid, and was the subject of a number of sightings and encounters over the years. The Fouke Monster was later immortalized in the movie "The Legend of Boggy Creek."

These are just a few examples of the many famous Sasquatch sightings that have occurred over the years. While some may dismiss these encounters as hoaxes or misidentifications, others believe that they provide compelling evidence for the existence of Bigfoot.

There are several ancient myths and legends from around the world that some people believe could be connected to Bigfoot. For example, Native American cultures have many stories about creatures that are similar to Sasquatch. These stories often describe creatures that live in the forest and are said to be very tall and covered in hair.

One famous legend comes from the Haida people of British Columbia. According to their tradition, there is a creature called the Gogit or Kushtaka, which is said to be a shape-shifter that can take on the form of a man or a giant otter. Some people believe that this legend could be based on actual sightings of Bigfoot.

Similarly, there are legends from other parts of the world that describe large, hairy creatures that live in the woods. In Australia, there is the Yowie, which is said to be a hominid creature that resembles Bigfoot. In Nepal, there is the Yeti, also known as the

Abominable Snowman, which is said to live in the Himalayas.

Throughout history and around the world, there have been many legends of large, hairy, humanoid creatures that share similarities with Bigfoot. In Europe, there is the legend of the "wild man," also known as the "woodwose," who is said to inhabit the forests and mountains. In Australia, the Aboriginal people have long told stories of the "yowie," a creature that is described as a large, hairy hominid.

In North America, Native American tribes have their own legends of "wild men" or "hairy men," such as the "omah" of the Cheyenne people and the "skookum" of the Chinook people. These legends often describe creatures that are very similar to Bigfoot, with accounts of large, hairy, bipedal beings that live in the wilderness.

It's possible that some of these legends and myths may have been inspired by real sightings of Bigfoot or other undiscovered primate species. Alternatively, they may simply be the result of human imagination and the universal fear of the unknown. Whatever the case may be, these stories add to the mystery and intrigue surrounding the elusive Sasquatch.

CHAPTER 9: FINAL THOUGHTS AND CONCLUSIONS

As we come to the end of this book, it's clear that the Sasquatch or Bigfoot remains an elusive creature that continues to fascinate and intrigue people all over the world. Despite the lack of concrete evidence, the sheer number of sightings and reports cannot be ignored, and it's safe to say that the mystery of the Sasquatch will continue to be a topic of discussion and research for many years to come.

Throughout this book, we've explored the history of Sasquatch sightings, the research techniques used to find evidence of its existence, the myths and legends surrounding the creature, and its place in popular culture. We've heard from both skeptics and proponents of its existence, and while opinions differ, it's clear that there is a genuine desire to uncover the truth about Bigfoot.

As technology advances, and the scientific community becomes more involved in the search for Sasquatch, we may one day have the proof we need to confirm its existence. Until then, the mystery and legend of the Sasquatch will continue to captivate our imagination and inspire us to explore the unknown.

In conclusion, the Sasquatch remains one of the most fascinating and elusive creatures in modern history. Its legend spans centuries, and its place in popular culture is cemented. Regardless of whether or not it exists, the hunt for Sasquatch will continue to captivate us, inspire us, and keep us searching for the unknown.

Disclaimer:

The information contained in this book is intended to be educational and informative. While every effort has been made to ensure that the content is accurate and up-to-date, the author and publisher make no guarantees regarding the completeness, accuracy, or suitability of the information presented.

The content in this book is based on a combination of research, personal experience, and anecdotal evidence, and should not be construed as medical, legal, or professional advice. The author and publisher are not liable for any damages or losses that may arise from the use or reliance on the information presented in this book.

Additionally, some of the illustrations in this book were generated using artificial intelligence (AI) and are intended to be artistic representations of the Bigfoot. While we have made every effort to ensure that these illustrations are respectful and accurate representations of the Bigfoot, they are not intended to be scientifically accurate depictions of this cryptid. The opinions and interpretations of the Skunk Ape presented in this book are based on folklore and personal accounts, and may not reflect the viewpoints of all readers.

This disclaimer is intended to provide clarity and transparency regarding the content of the book and the use of AI-generated illustrations, and to protect both the author and publisher from any legal liability or damages that may arise from the use of the information presented in this book.